A Planet Beyond

Written by Tom Bradman
Illustrated by Aga Maszota

Words to look out for ...

alter (*verb*)
alters, altering, altered
To alter something is to change it.

amend (*verb*)
amends, amending, amended
to change something in order to improve it

conceal (*verb*)
conceals, concealing, concealed
to hide something or keep it secret

disadvantage (*noun*)
something that is unhelpful or that causes a problem

establish (*verb*)
establishes, establishing, established
To establish an organization or group is to start it.

indicate (*verb*)
indicates, indicating, indicated
To indicate something is to point it out or show it.

process (*verb*)
processes, processing, processed
To process something is to deal with it by doing a series of things.

specific (*adjective*)
definite or particular

Chapter 1

The journey had been a long one for Manu.

A whole year in space.

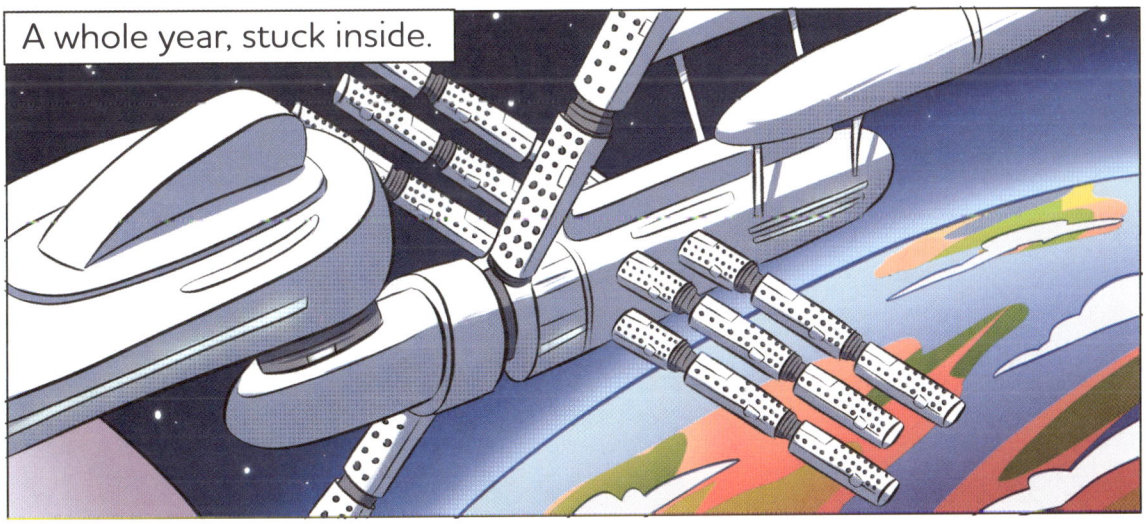

A whole year, stuck inside.

Finally, Manu had arrived.

The first town had already been established.

The new people on the planet were having trouble growing food there.

Manu's parents had come to solve the problem.

Now Manu was entering this unknown world with them.

To establish an organization or group is to start it.

Specific means definite or particular.

Chapter 2

To conceal something is to hide it or keep it secret.

You are at a disadvantage when something is unhelpful or when something is causing a problem.

16   To indicate something is to point it out or show it.

To alter something is to change it.

Chapter 3

A few weeks later ...

"How are the little ones doing today?"

"They're not so little any more!"

"They're eating all of the fungus."

"It looks like we're going to have a good harvest after all!"

As the creatures grew, so did the farm. It was able to supply food for everyone who needed it.

Over time, more was learnt about the creatures.

Farming methods were amended to protect them and their planet.

The people continued to find ways to live on the planet, in peace with nature.

To amend something is to change it in order to improve it.